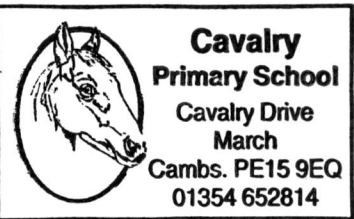

CHERRYTREE BOOKS

THE LIVING PLANET
THE LAND

Edited by Tom Mariner

A Cherrytree Book

Adapted by A S Publishing from
El Paisaje © Parramon Ediciones S.A. 1996
Text: Miquel Àngel Gibert
Illustrations: Lidia di Blasi
Design: Beatriz Seoane

This edition first published in 1997
by Cherrytree Press Ltd
a subsidiary of
The Chivers Company Ltd
Windsor Bridge Road
Bath BA2 3AX

© Cherrytree Press Ltd 1997

British Library Cataloguing in Publication Data
The land. – (The living planet)
  1. Earth – Juvenile literature
  I. Mariner, Tom
  550

ISBN 0 7451 5316 X

Typeset by Dorchester Typesetting Group Ltd, Dorset
Printed in Spain

All rights reserved. No part of this publication may be reproduced, stored in a retrieval system, or transmitted, in any form or by any means, without the prior permission in writing of the publisher, nor be otherwise circulated in any form of binding or cover other than that in which it is published and without a similar condition including this condition being imposed on the subsequent purchaser.

A bird's-eye view of a coastal landscape showing how the land is carved by rivers and streams and the coast by the sea itself.

Contents

The living landscape	4	The northern forests	20
The shape of the land	6	Life in the tundra	22
Erosion	8	Marshes, swamps and mangroves	24
Climate and vegetation	10		
The abundant rainforests	12	Changing the face of the land	26
The savannas, home of the herds	14	Making mountains and habitats	28
Survival in the desert	16	Glossary	30
Grasslands, where bison roamed	18	Index	32

THE LAND

The Living Landscape

WHAT DO YOU see when you look around you? City streets, open country, rolling hills, the sea? The shape of the land depends mostly on the rock that lies beneath it. Natural processes over millions of years have shaped the rock into what we see today; mountains or valleys, plains or hills, cliffs or sandy beaches. The surface features of the landscape are largely determined by climate; for climate determines what plants and animals can live in any place.

Whatever the natural vegetation may be – forest, grassland or scrub – nearly everywhere there will be animals. Most will stay safely out of sight, but others, such as reindeer in the snowy Arctic tundra or eagles soaring high over rocky ledges, will add a living presence in the landscape.

The character of the landscape depends on the rocks beneath it, the plant and animal life that it supports, and the changes that people have made to it.

The most significant changes to the landscape have been made by human beings. Throughout history they have cut down forests, drained swamps, ploughed grasslands and altered the character of vast tracts of land. More recently they have built dams, causing river valleys to flood. They have hacked out huge holes in the ground to get building stone for towns and roads.

THE LAND

PRECAMBRIAN 4600-590* PALAEOZOIC 590-248 *Millions of years ago

MESOZOIC   Triassic 248-213   Jurassic 213-144   Cretaceous 144-65

The earth formed around 4600 million years ago. If we could travel backwards in time, we would see that the landscape has constantly changed. The continents are continually on the move, inching apart or together in different parts of the world. The shape of the land changes too. Mountain ranges that were once tall are now mere hills. Climates have changed. Several times the world has grown so cold that ice sheets have spread across lands that are now tropical. All the time, the animals and plants have been changing.

People have been on earth for a relatively short length of time. Before they appeared, other animals dominated the earth. We know about them from their fossils, traces of living things left in the rocks. Geologists use fossils to identify the ages of rocks. They divide the time into eras and periods. In Precambrian times life was confined to the sea. During the Palaeozoic era fish evolved, followed by amphibians and reptiles. During the Mesozoic dinosaurs ruled the earth. Mammals, including humans, became dominant during the Cenozoic, the era in which we live.

Life forms and landscapes evolve all the time. One of the most important influences is climate.

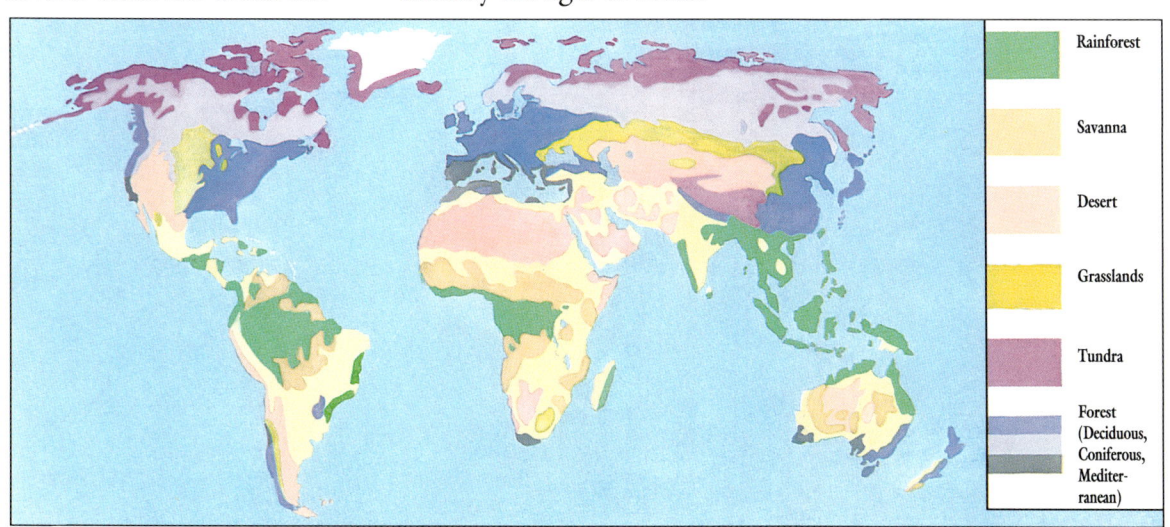

Rainforest
Savanna
Desert
Grasslands
Tundra
Forest (Deciduous, Coniferous, Mediterranean)

5

THE LAND

THE SHAPE OF THE LAND

Mountains and lakes, rolling hills, flat plains and rocky outcrops are features of an ever-changing landscape. The earth's surface is cracked into 'plates' that float on a layer of semi-molten rock. Forces in this layer cause the plates to move. In one place they collide and in another they move apart. Where they collide, the land may buckle up into mountains, called fold mountains.

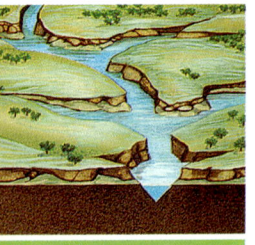

The shape of the land is created by forces within the earth but is continually changed by the action of weathering, water and other natural agents on the surface.

As fast as mountains form, they begin to be broken down by natural forces. Rain, wind, frost and ice carve the rocky surface into a variety of shapes and over millions of years wear it flat. Rivers carve valleys and carry the broken rock particles – sediment – to the sea. The sediment settles in layers on the sea bed and in time forms new rock, which may later be raised up by earth movements.

6

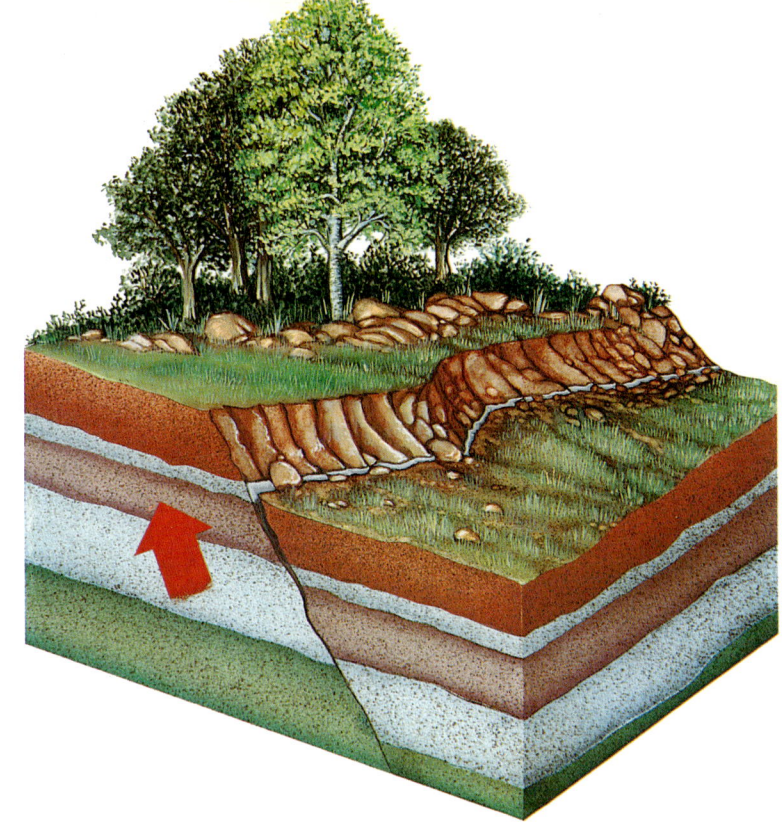

THE LAND

In some places when plates meet head-on or are moving past each other, the rocks do not fold but break. These breaks are called faults. The rocks on each side of the fault may be forced up or down. When two faults occur parallel to each other, the rock between may be forced up to form a flat-topped block mountain, or it may be forced down to form a rift valley. Sometimes parts of the valley fill with water to form lakes.

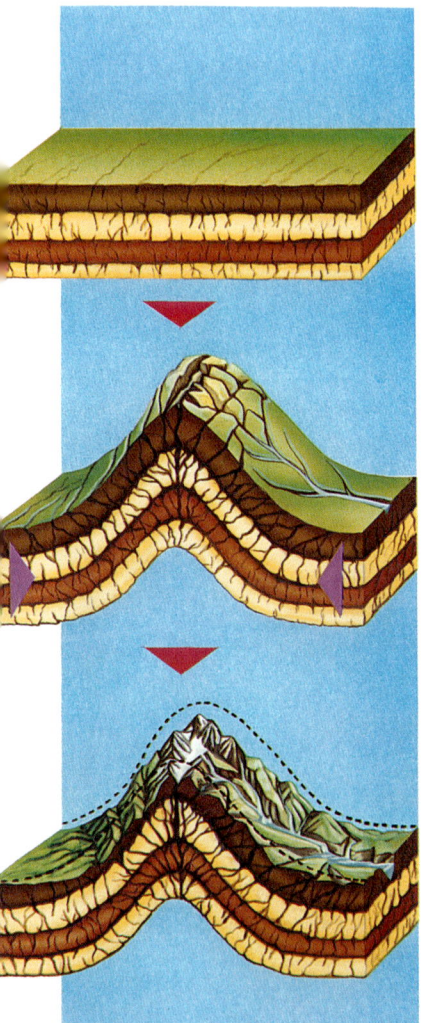

Sudden movements along a fault can cause devastating earthquakes. Many severe quakes occur along transform faults where two plates are moving past each other but have got jammed together. The pressure mounts until suddenly the rocks snap and the plates shift with a jerk.

Volcanoes also occur where plates move against each other. Magma pours out of volcanoes as lava, solidifies into new rock and in time builds up into mountains. Where plates move apart, under the sea, magma wells up to form new rock. In some places the edge of one plate slides down under another into the magma and the rock is destroyed. The continuous destruction of old rock and emergence of new rock is called the rock cycle.

Earth movements create mountains, rivers carve valleys and rocks are worn down and carried to the sea.

7

THE LAND

EROSION

THE SURFACE OF the earth is constantly under attack. It is worn away, or eroded, by weathering (extremes of temperature and chemical action) and the forces of wind, water and ice. Sooner or later all the rock fragments that result from erosion in one place are deposited in another. They may be moved downhill by gravity, blown by the wind or swept away by rivers to end up in the sea.

On sea coasts waves carrying sand and pebbles endlessly pound the shore. They cut into a cliff face and weaken its base. Eventually the rock, soil and vegetation above collapse, leaving a bare cliff. Where the rock is soft, the sea may carve caves. When waves pound both sides of a headland, they may wear through the rock between two caves, causing a natural arch.

On land the wind acts like a sandblaster. It picks up dust and sand and hurls them at the rocks. Because the wind cannot lift them high, the rock is worn down more at ground level than higher up, which results in strange shapes.

Land surfaces are shaped by erosion. Rocks and soil slide downhill or are carried down by wind, ice or water.

These strange pillars are shaped by wind and running water. Boulders of hard rock lying on the ground have protected the rock beneath from erosion.

THE LAND

On high mountains the snow never melts. It builds up in layers many metres deep. The fresh snow weighs down on the snow below, compacting it into ice. As the ice thickens, it becomes heavier and begins to move downhill under its own weight. It becomes a river of ice called a glacier. Rocks embedded in the ice act as scrapers, gouging out the surrounding rock in a steep-sided U-shaped valley.

The scenery in many desert regions results from ancient glaciers and rivers. Rainstorms in deserts are rare, but may be violent enough to cause instant rivers that sweep away the surface sand. Wind-blown sand continues the work of the rain by scouring everything in its path. Hard rocks remain after softer rocks have been worn away leaving a landscape of rounded rocks and isolated flat-topped hills.

Near its source, a mountain torrent carves out a steep-sided, funnel-shaped valley typical of mountain landscapes everywhere.

Rivers often start where glaciers end. Torrents of melted snow, swollen with rain, sweep downhill carrying loose rocks that carve a V-shaped valley. As it flows, a river picks up pebbles, sand and mud. Nearer its mouth it loses pace and gradually drops its load. Whatever reaches the sea is spread along the shore by sea currents to form beaches, some of which are backed by lines of dunes.

9

THE LAND

CLIMATE AND VEGETATION

DURING THE ICE ages, polar ice sheets spread out over the globe. While northern lands were covered with ice, places that are now hot and dry had mild temperate climates. The Sahara was warm enough to support wild animals, people and cattle. Then, about 10,000 years ago, the climate became hotter. The ice melted and the once fertile lands farther south eventually became desert.

The Sahara 5000 years ago

Because of the curve of the earth, the sun's rays are most effective at the equator and less so at the poles.

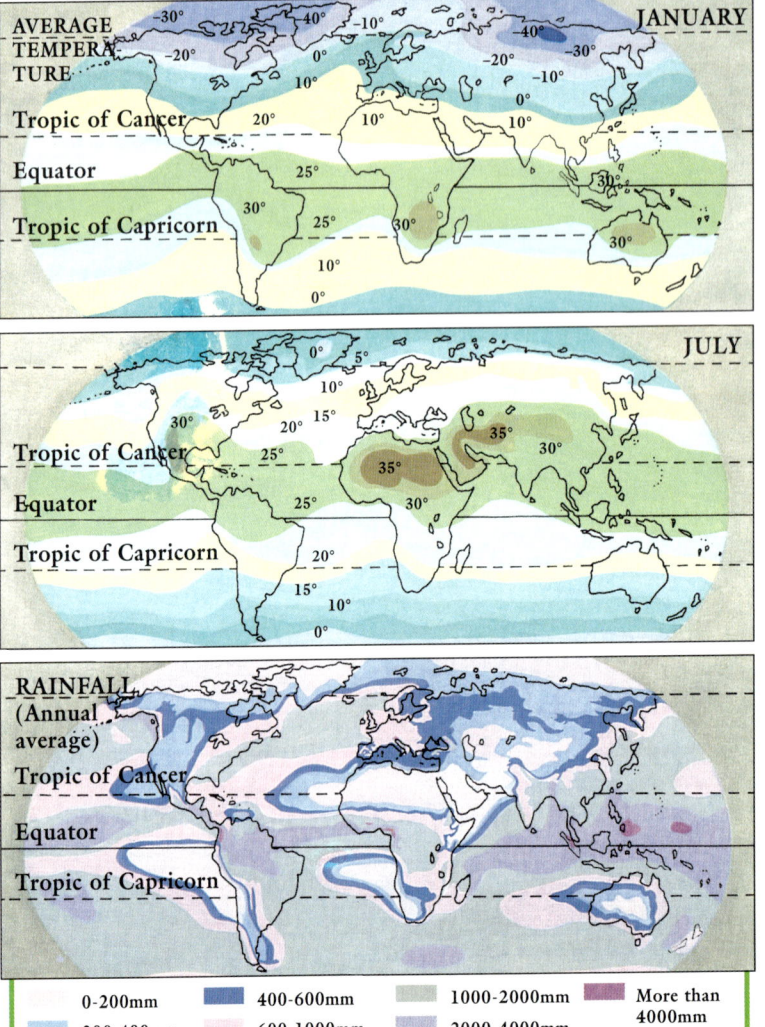

Climate is determined primarily by the sun. Near the equator, the sun is almost directly overhead so the lands there receive the strongest sunlight. Near the poles, the sun's rays hit the earth at an angle and are spread out over a greater area, making the land cooler. The heat from the ground at the equator warms the air and makes it rise. As it rises, the air cools. The water vapour in the cooled air condenses and falls back to earth as rain. The mass of air, now cool and dry, spreads out north and south of the equator. Around latitudes 30°N and 30°S, near the tropics of Cancer and Capricorn, the cool air sinks, becoming warmer as it descends. Warm air can hold more water vapour than cold air so there is no rainfall and vast areas of land in those regions are hot deserts.

10

THE LAND

Plants need water and sunlight to grow well, so the vegetation and animal life in any region depend on the climate. The equatorial climate is hot and wet all year round, so plants grow thick and fast, forming dense rainforests. Desert climates are hot and dry all year. Few plants can grow in these conditions, so the land is bare rock or shifting sand dunes.

It is not only distance from the equator that determines climate. Distance from the sea is also important. Ocean currents increase or decrease the temperature of coastal lands. Water also warms up and cools down more slowly than land. As a result inland areas have warmer summers and colder winters with less rainfall. These conditions have created vast grassy plains with few trees.

Plant life is most vigorous and most varied in areas of great heat and high rainfall.

Altitude also affects climate. Temperature falls by about one degree Celsius for every 100m climbed, so as you go up a mountain you pass through increasingly cool climates. The wettest areas are found on coasts where prevailing winds have come great distances over the sea. These winds drop their moisture as they rise over coastal mountains. Now dry, they continue on and cause deserts to form farther inland.

11

THE LAND
THE ABUNDANT RAINFORESTS

Emergents

Canopy

Understorey

Forest floor

Tropical rainforests flourish at the equator, the only place where heat and water are available all year round.

NOWHERE ON earth is plant and animal life so abundant as in tropical rainforests. The plants grow closely together because the water and warmth they need is available all year round. The forest has several layers. The tallest trees are called emergents. Below them is a dense canopy of tree crowns, and below them an understorey of smaller trees, shrubs and ferns. The lowest layer is the shady forest floor.

In the struggle to reach the light, woody vines called lianas clamber up the trees and burst into leaf only when they have reached the canopy. Other forest plants, the epiphytes, never touch the ground. They root on high branches where they live off nutrients dissolved in rainwater and on decaying leaves that drift down from the canopy above. Orchids are the most well known epiphytes. Mosses, lichens and fungi also grow on the other plants and on the forest floor.

Plant life in tropical rainforests is more diverse than anywhere else on earth. Scientists believe that about half of the world's estimated 4.5 million plant and animal species live in these hot, damp regions. In one square kilometre, 200 different trees may flourish. As many as 100 different kinds of plant may climb up or grow on a single tree. The Amazon rainforest in Brazil covers 6 million sq km.

Rainforest soils tend to be infertile. Nutrients are quickly used by growing plants or washed away by the rain. The plants take their nourishment from the never-ending rain of decaying vegetation that falls from the canopy. Even the great trees have shallow roots in order to feed on the nutrients lying on the surface.

The diversity of animal life in the rainforests is as rich as that of the plants. One-tenth of the world's bird species live in the Brazilian forest and some 2500 kinds of fish swim in the Amazon river. The tree layers provide a variety of habitats. In the canopy, monkeys, snakes and sloths move through the branches alongside parrots, toucans and hummingbirds. On the ground are ants and snakes and the strange armadillo. Big predators like the jaguar stalk through the trees, while insects are found at all levels.

Every time a giant forest tree falls a gap opens in the canopy. Seeds lying dormant on the floor quickly take root and grow towards the precious sunlight.

THE LAND

The Savannas, Home of the Herds

SAVANNAS ARE tropical grasslands with widely scattered trees and shrubs. They are the home of the elephant and herds of other grazing animals that feed on clumps of grass and gather at water holes. Most savannas experience daytime temperatures that rarely fall below 20°C and the rainy season is short. So getting enough water is important for both plants and animals.

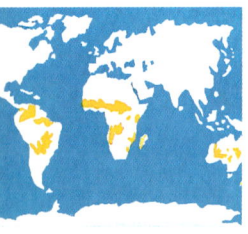

Savannas cover nearly 40% of Africa and vast regions of South America and Australia.

Baobab   Acacia

The grass has thick blades that conserve moisture. In dry places it is only a few centimetres high, but in wetter areas it may be three metres. There is too little water for most trees to grow but acacia and baobab trees have ways of surviving drought. The acacia has spiny leaves and its roots go down deep enough to reach moisture in the ground. Baobabs store water in their huge, spongy trunks.

January February March April May June July August September October November December

THE LAND

Every year, as the long dry season ends, huge fires sweep across the African savannas, their flames licking through the carpet of dead, brown grass. Burning gives new life to the savanna. It prevents trees from spreading at the expense of valuable grass. The ashes of the burnt grass enrich the soil and help new grass to grow. The seeds and roots of the grasses are untouched by the flames and are ready to spring to life again when the rains come. Then, the daily downpours turn the grass green and let flowers bloom. Mature acacia trees that have survived the flames are covered with yellow blossom.

The new grass is grazed by different animals in succession. Zebras bite off the coarse tops of the grasses. Wildebeests follow and chew the lower and more tender parts of the grass down to the ground. Finally gazelles nibble the green shoots that spring from the base of the stems. Giraffes browse on the trees above.

Every year at certain times the herds of the African savannas migrate to richer pastures, often travelling hundreds of kilometres. Wherever they go, they are followed by animals that prey upon them – lions, leopards, cheetahs, hyenas and jackals.

Rainy seasons twice a year bring renewal to the parched, and often burnt, grasslands. Animals migrate to take advantage of the fresh grass.

15

THE LAND

SURVIVAL IN THE DESERT

HOT DESERTS have an almost unbearable climate. Temperatures may rise to 40°C by day and drop to freezing point at night. Water is scarce or non-existent. In parts of the Sahara in Africa and the Atacama in South America rain may not fall for years, then a sudden storm may produce a flash flood. Yet life manages to survive. Both animals and plants have adapted to the conditions.

Some plants are drought evaders. Their seeds lie on the ground waiting for rain. When enough comes they spring into life and within a few weeks flower and scatter their seeds. Other plants are drought resisters. Cactuses have long shallow roots that collect water over a large area to store in their fleshy stems. Their waxy skin and spines retain the moisture and make them hard for animals to eat.

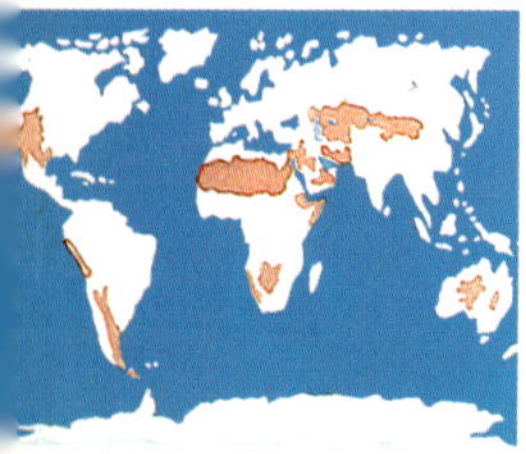

Hot deserts occupy about one-seventh of the world's land surface. Many are a sea of barren sand, but others support a variety of plants.

Wind and water shape the desert surface. A quarter of the world's deserts are covered with sand, which the winds pile up into dunes. Elsewhere the winds sweep away all the loose sand, leaving bare rock. Rain from rare but violent cloudbursts scours deep, straight-sided valleys in the desert floor. These normally dry river beds are called wadis or arroyos.

16

THE LAND

An oasis is a green and fertile place in the desert, where there is always enough water to keep plants and animals alive. The water comes from springs, underground streams or wells. In some places water from hills or mountains seeps through permeable rocks deep underground and then surfaces. Date palms, with their highly nutritious fruit, commonly grow around oases in the deserts of North Africa.

At night the desert comes alive. Lizards and snakes and small mammals, such as kit foxes and kangaroo rats, hide under stones or in burrows during the day. They come out only in the cool of the night. They take care to avoid poisonous scorpions and snakes. The Arabian camel can go for a week without drinking. Fat in its hump gives it an indirect water supply.

When rain comes, millions of insects emerge from eggs and grubs. Like the plants, they must be quick to breed and lay their eggs before they die from lack of moisture.

The animals in the picture would not all be found in the same desert. Those to the left of the tall saguaro cactus come from North American deserts. Those on the right come from African and Asian deserts.

Many desert animals have adaptations that help them survive. The fennec fox has big ears that give it excellent hearing for hunting at night. They also radiate heat and help keep it cool by day.

17

THE LAND

Grasslands, where Bison Roamed

PRAIRIE

ONCE THE prairies of North America were a sea of tall waving grasses where great herds of bison roamed. Today the rolling plains are planted with wheat or maize. The prairies, the pampas of South America, the veld of southern Africa and the steppes of Eurasia are the great temperate grasslands of the world. Like the savannas they have a long dry season which restricts the growth of trees.

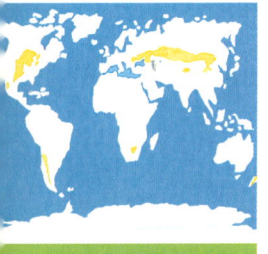

The great grasslands lie in the heart of the continents far from the sea.

The grass grows as high as the rainfall allows. In the prairies it may be two metres tall, but in steppe regions, it may be less than 25 centimetres high. Though summers are hot, winters are cold. The climate on the steppes is particularly harsh with freezing winters and baking hot summers. Lack of water allows only short, often scanty, grass to grow. Steppe is the natural vegetation of much of North America as well as Eurasia.

STEPPE

18

The rich, dark soil of the prairies is more fertile than that of the steppes. It contains more humus, which forms like compost from the decay of vegetable material. The greater rainfall on the prairies allows more grass to grow. The natural decay of the dense mat of its long roots makes the soil fertile. The relatively thin vegetation of the steppe makes the soil thinner and poorer.

PRAIRIE IN SUMMER

Only the least fertile and inhospitably cold areas of grassland retain their natural vegetation and wildlife today. Most have been turned into farmland. Wheat is grown on prairie and steppe alike, though the yield from the former is greater. Where the land is not right for crops, cattle are grazed. The pampas and the veld have rich prairie soils suitable for growing crops and raising livestock.

PRAIRIE IN WINTER

Most of the world's natural grasslands are now used for growing wheat or grazing cattle.

Like the bison, most animals that live, or once lived, on the prairies are herbivores. The antelope-like pronghorn and the jack rabbit run to escape their enemies. The prairie dog stays safe in tunnels below the ground. Its holes are also used by the burrowing owl, while the prairie chicken, a type of grouse, nests among the grasses. Everywhere there are insects, especially butterflies and grasshoppers.

THE LAND

THE NORTHERN FORESTS

MOST OF THE world's temperate forests are in the northern hemisphere. Thousands of years ago nearly the whole of Europe was one vast forest, as was much of northern North America and Asia. As soon as human beings had the tools, they cut the trees down for firewood, timber and farmland. Even so, much natural forest still remains.

- Temperate
- Mediterranean
- Boreal

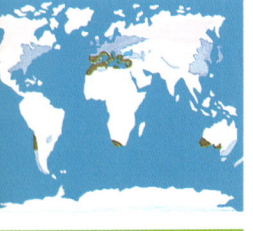

The temperate regions of the earth were once covered with trees, but most of the forests have been cleared to provide timber and make way for farms, roads and cities.

The types of trees that grow vary with the climate. In the north are evergreen coniferous trees, which can withstand long bitter winters. To the south are broad-leaved deciduous trees that shed their leaves once a year.

In Mediterranean woodlands the trees are mostly evergreens with small tough leaves that can cope with strong summer sunlight and shortage of water. Similar vegetation is found in California and in some coastal regions in the southern hemisphere.

Beneath the taller trees are bushes and shrubs and below them undergrowth. In clearings the light enables a wealth of flowers to bloom. Unlike the oak trees that grow farther north, the cork oak has evergreen leaves. Its thick bark is used to make corks.

In areas of the forest that are undisturbed, many animals make their homes. The largest are the deer. The fiercest are foxes and wild cats like the lynx that prey on rabbits, mice and other small animals. The wild boar is also ferocious though it feeds only on vegetable matter.

Cork oak

20

The appearance of deciduous woodland changes with the seasons. In winter the branches are bare. In spring the leaves begin to bud as the temperature increases. The sun shines through the tree tops and flowers bloom on the forest floor. By summer time the leaves are so broad that not enough light penetrates for shrubs or flowers to grow under the canopy. The leaves of great trees, such as beech, oak, elm, chestnut and ash, soak up the sun, giving the trees energy to produce their fruits and seeds and make enough food to nourish the trees until spring. By autumn the leaves are ready to drop, but before they do they change from green to a magnificent array of reds and yellows. All year round, songbirds and small mammals find plenty of food and shelter amongst the trees.

Almost a third of the world's remaining forests are coniferous. Conifers are also grown in plantations to provide softwood for buildings, furniture and paper.

DECIDUOUS TREES

Spring	Summer	Autumn	Winter

In a coniferous, or boreal, forest the trees grow tall and straight. Most conifers, including pines, firs and cedars, are conical in shape. Their evergreen leaves are like needles with a waxy coating that prevents them losing moisture and helps them survive long periods of cold. Their branches do not break in heavy snow because they bend easily and allow the snow to slip off.

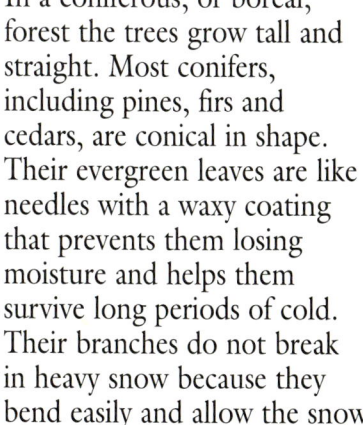

THE LAND

21

THE LAND

LIFE IN THE TUNDRA

THE TUNDRA is a region of treeless plains in far northern North America, Europe and Asia. For most of the year the temperature stays below freezing point. Freezing winds blow and snow covers the ground throughout the long dark winter. Summers are short and cool but there is enough sunlight and heat for a carpet of low-growing plants to burst into flower and make their seeds.

The main areas of tundra are around the Arctic ocean between the tree line and the region of perpetual ice around the pole. Tundra conditions also exist on high mountains.

The tundra plants are mostly grasses, mosses, lichens and plants called sedges. They form ground-hugging hummocks that can resist the wind. No trees grow because of the intensely cold winter winds and the permanently frozen soil, called permafrost, below the surface. The summer temperatures thaw only the top layer of soil, the subsoil remains locked in ice.

PLANT LAYER
SOIL LAYER
PERMAFROST

The ice prevents the melted snow from draining away so the thawed summer soil is always wet. Hollows fill with water so that the landscape looks like an immense meadow dotted with pools and streams. Caribou and reindeer that have sheltered in the coniferous forests to the south during the winter return in herds many thousands strong to browse on the tundra's fresh green herbage.

22

Seasonal changes are spectacular on the tundra. The plants must cram a complete life cycle into the short growing season. Some grow, flower and produce seeds within a month. Along with the migrating herds, seabirds and waterfowl arrive to feed and nest among the new grass and flowers.

At the first suggestion of winter the migrants go south, leaving only lemmings, arctic hares and foxes and the sturdy musk oxen to live through the savage tundra winter. Many of these creatures are preyed upon by the polar bear which comes south to hunt. When winter comes the foxes and hares grow thick white coats, and the ptarmigans exchange their striped brown feathers for white ones. Their white winter coats camouflage them in the snow.

SUMMER

WINTER

Few animals can stay alive all year round in the tundra. The lemming survives in a labyrinth of tunnels under the snow feeding on plant roots and shoots.

Because the tundra's climate is so forbidding and the land is unsuitable for agriculture, it has been left largely unspoilt. But the mining of the Arctic's rich deposits of oil, gas, iron ore, coal and other minerals poses a threat. Already a pipeline built to carry oil and gas scars the landscape, and tracks made by vehicles forty years ago are still visible today because the vegetation recovers so slowly.

THE LAND

Marshes, Swamps and Mangroves

BOG, MARSH, swamp and fen are some of the names given to wet, spongy land where the water level remains near or above the surface. Freshwater wetlands occur on the margins of lakes, in places where there is excess rainfall, melting snow or flooding rivers, or where underground water reaches the surface. Saltwater wetlands, such as mangrove swamps, are found on coasts flooded by the sea.

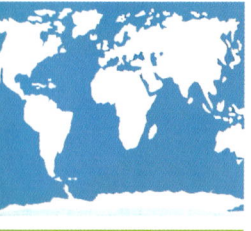

Wetlands are found all over the world. Many of them are protected habitats but others are in danger from developers who drain the land and build on it.

Temperate wetlands are havens for water birds, particularly those that migrate. One of the most spectacular migrants is the white stork. After spending the summer in the low countries, the storks fly south to warmer climates. They set off in autumn and many pause to rest and feed in wetlands on the coasts of Spain and Portugal before flying on to spend the winter in Africa.

Freshwater marshes are rich in grasses, rushes and reeds and in aquatic plants. Water lilies like clear water. Their roots send long stalks up from the bottom and their wide leaves float on the surface. Swamps have trees and shrubs. Bogs and fens are found in northern climates. Their soil is acidic and the plants are mostly mosses. Decayed matter forms thick layers of peat.

THE LAND

Saltwater wetlands form in estuaries where the tide rises high enough to flood the riverbanks. The river slows down as it meets the seawater. At high tide it overflows its banks and drops the mud and silt it has been carrying on to the mudflats by its banks. Carried by the wind, seeds of hardy spartina grass fall on the mud. When they germinate, their roots grow and form a network that spreads out and anchors the wet and shifting soil. As a result sea plantain and other plants that are less tolerant of salt and of being submerged can take up residence. Their roots bind the soil even more and gradually a community of plants is established that can cope with the general wetness and twice-daily flooding by seawater.

Mangrove swamps are found on tropical coasts. Mangrove trees send down long stilt-like roots from their branches. The roots form a network that traps and binds the mud and silt below the water and holds the branches and crown above it. The seeds often put out roots while the fruit is still on the tree. The seed root trails in the water until the fruit falls in the water. Then the root tip strikes mud and begins to grow a new tree. Mangrove swamps are home to many fish, birds and the saltwater crocodile.

Spring tide level every two weeks

High tide level twice a day

Wetlands are a refuge for many animals, including the saltwater crocodile. Instead of being drained many marshes are now being conserved.

25

Changing the Face of the Land

THERE ARE FEW places left on earth that have not been changed by human beings. Landscapes that have grown naturally over thousands of years are transformed in weeks or months. In densely populated parts of the developed world the natural vegetation has long since disappeared, transformed into cities and farmland. Today, in many of the poorest parts of the world this process is being repeated.

When the great tropical rainforest is cleared for cultivation, the land soon becomes infertile and the soil is not good enough for growing crops or for pasture.

Huge tracts of tropical rainforest are felled every year for timber and to provide new land for farming – in the mistaken belief that the forest soil is fertile. But of course the luxuriant growth of the forest results from the trees absorbing nutrients before they have a chance of enriching the soil. When people grow crops on the cleared land, the soil is soon exhausted. Burning the forest down creates rough grazing land, but cattle quickly strip away the grass and shrubs that replaced the trees. When new pasture is needed the farmers who first cleared the forest move on to cut or burn down more trees and the process is repeated. The soil in the abandoned areas is then left bare and unprotected. Heavy tropical rain forms deep gullies and washes away the topsoil. In this way, tropical forest becomes wasteland.

THE LAND

Lightning causes some fires on the African savannas, but others are started deliberately by people who want to graze their animals or cultivate the land. Stripped of its natural vegetation, the land cannot support the wild animals, and because of the climate crops do not thrive. Goats strip the trees of their leaves and kill them. When the rains come, they wash away the soil and turn the land into desert.

During this century, more and more people have moved away from the land. In parts of the world where the soil is poor, farmers struggle to survive. Their children move to cities in search of work and live in ever-spreading suburbs and shanty towns. Towns and road systems in the developed world grow too, and you can travel for miles through the urban landscape without seeing a patch of green.

All over the world forests of buildings have replaced centuries-old forests of trees. People have totally transformed natural landscapes into totally artificial townscapes.

Precious forests are not just cut down, some are killed by pollution. Power stations, factories and cars pour out smoke containing chemicals that turn to acid if dissolved in rain. This acid can be lethal for trees. Building taller chimneys allows the winds to blow the smoke farther away, so that pollution from one country may acidify the rain that falls on forests in another.

27

Making Mountains and Habitats

Use modelling clay to make a landscape. Work some clay into three rectangles. Lay them on a board between two pieces of wood, then push the sides together. The layers of clay should fold upwards forming mountains, in the same way as real mountains are formed by colossal pressures on layers of rock.

Do the same with more clay until you have a model landscape. You may have to cheat by working the clay into peaks and valleys with your fingers. If you want the mountains to look old and rounded, imitate the action of the wind and rain by sandpapering them. Then take your model outside or to a place where it doesn't matter if you make things wet. Spray water over the mountains so that it falls like rain.

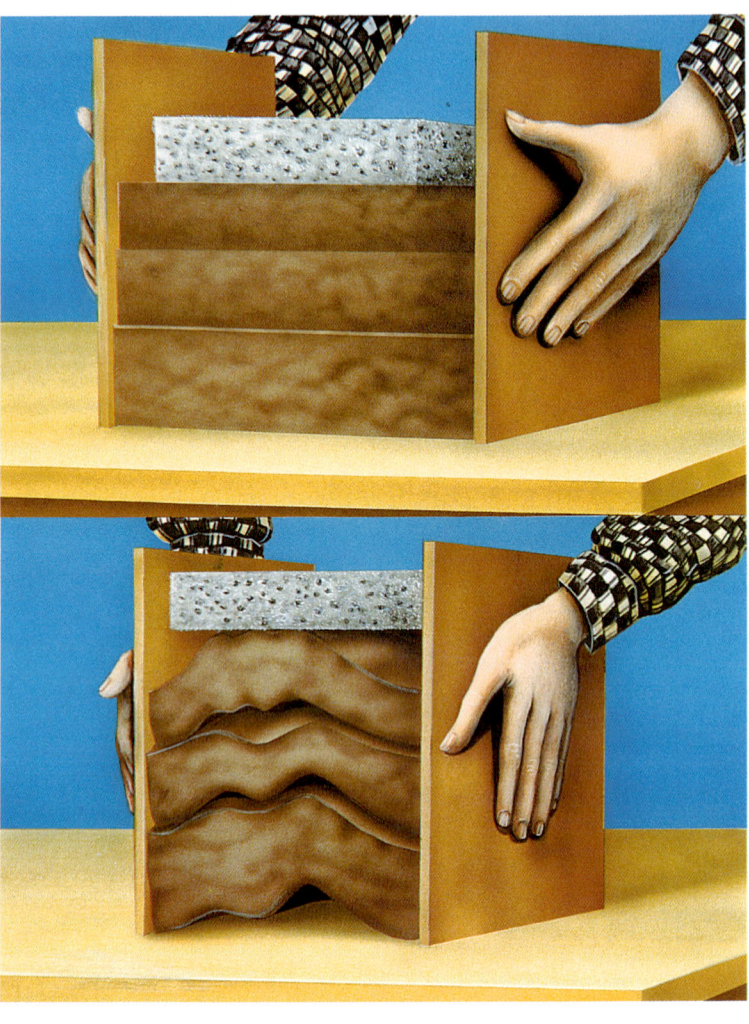

Watch the water as it runs down the mountainsides and collects in the valleys to form rivers. See how loose pieces of clay on the mountains are washed into the rivers and laid down on the flat land below. Once the relief is as you want it, let it dry. Using waterproof paints, paint the model with blue rivers, green plains and snowy white mountain tops.

PLANT A MOUNTAIN
Make a second, larger model of a single mountain and the land around it. Then paint the natural vegetation on it. Just as the climate and vegetation change as you go from the equator to the poles, so they change as you go up a mountain. If the valleys and lowlands around your mountain are planted with crops, the lowest slopes of the mountain will have shrubs and deciduous trees on them, which will merge higher up into a band of coniferous trees. Then, at the tree line, the trees will stop and give way to alpine meadows with low-growing plants like those of the tundra. Further up still these plants will become scantier, until at last the rocks are bare. Above the bare rocks, beyond the snow line, there is a region of perpetual ice and snow.

Snow and ice
SNOW LINE
Bare rock
Alpine meadows
TREE LINE
Coniferous trees
Deciduous trees
Farmland

CREATE A RAINFOREST
If you have a greenhouse you can grow plants that you would normally find only in a rainforest. For tropical orchids you need to reproduce the hot, sticky climate by giving them daily sunlight, a steady temperature above 23°C and spraying the leaves. Orchids can be expensive so get advice from a good book or an expert.

29

GLOSSARY

ADAPTATION Way in which animals and plants have evolved both physically and in behaviour to survive in their environment.
ARMADILLO Small mammal that has bands of bony armour round its body.
ARROYO Dried-up river bed that turns back into a river when it rains.
BISON Large wild ox, often called a buffalo in North America.
BLOCK MOUNTAIN Flat-topped mountain that has been forced up between parallel faults.
BOG Freshwater wetland with spongy, often peaty, ground.
BOREAL FOREST Coniferous forest.
CANOPY Dense leafy layer formed by the crowns (tops) of rainforest trees.
CONIFER Evergreen cone-bearing tree with needle-shaped leaves.
DECIDUOUS Describes any tree that sheds its leaves once a year.
DESERT Area with less than 25cm of rain a year. Deserts can be hot or cold.
DORMANT Sleeping, or in a state of suspended animation.
DUNES Piles of sand created in deserts and on beaches by the wind.
EMERGENT One of the tallest trees in a rainforest, which reaches above the canopy.

EPIPHYTE: A plant that grows on another plant or surface but gets its nourishment from the atmosphere.
EQUATOR Imaginary line round the middle of the earth.
EQUATORIAL Region that lies close to the equator.
ERA Division of geological time. Eras are divided into periods.
EROSION Wearing down of the land.
ESTUARY Mouth of a river where tidal saltwater meets the river's freshwater.
FAULT Break in rocks where one part has moved up or down or sideways.
FEN Marshy land, often covered with water.
FLASH FLOOD Flood caused by sudden rain in an area too dry for the water to drain away gently.
FOLD MOUNTAIN Mountain caused by the collision of crustal plates.
FRESHWATER Water in lakes and rivers.
GEOLOGIST Scientist who studies rocks.
GLACIER River of ice formed by snow falling on mountains.

GRASSLAND Temperate region whose natural vegetation is grass.
GULLY Channel worn by running water.
HABITAT Place where certain animals and plants normally live.
HEMISPHERE Half of a sphere. Used for the east-west and north-south halves of the earth.
HUMUS Rich part of the soil formed from decayed living matter.
ICE AGE Any of several long periods during which the earth's climate was so cold that huge sheets of ice covered large areas of the northern and southern hemispheres.
LATITUDE North-south position of any point on earth, shown by lines on the map. Lines of longitude show the east-west position.
LAVA Magma that has been cast out by a volcano.
LIANA Any of several types of climbing plants that grow in the tropics.

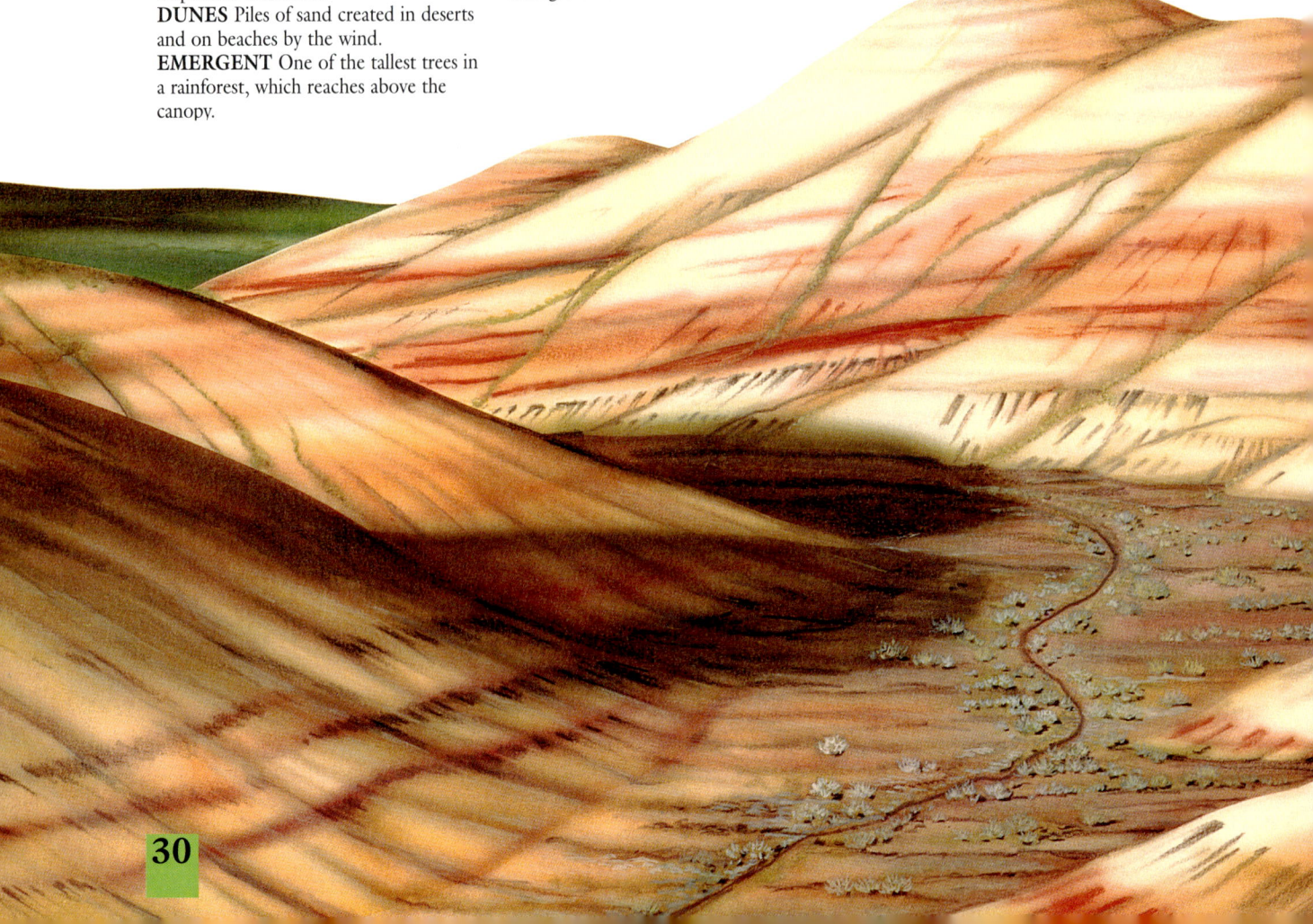

LICHEN Plant, consisting of a fungus and an alga, that grows on rocks, trees and other surfaces.
MANGROVE Tree found in swamps on tropical coasts.
MARSH Any area of wetland, such as a bog or fen.
MIGRATE To travel from one place to another, as wild deer and cattle and many birds do every year in search of food.
MOUNTAIN Raised areas of land, generally 700m or more above sea level. Lower uplands are called hills.
NUTRIENT Substance that provides nourishment for plants or animals.
OASIS Area of green in a desert where a spring or well gives a permanent water supply.
PAMPA Huge grassy plain in Argentina and other South American countries.
PEAT Decaying vegetable matter that builds up in wetlands. Over millions of years it turns to coal.
PERIOD Part of an era in geological time.
PERMAFROST Ground that is always frozen.
PERMEABLE Allowing water to pass through.
PLANTATION Land planted with a single crop, particularly trees.
PLATE One of eight large and many small pieces of the earth's crust.
POLE Point that marks the end (north or south) of the earth's axis, the imaginary line around which the planet spins.
PRAIRIE Grassy treeless plain of middle North America.
PREVAILING WIND Wind that blows most often from one direction.
PTARMIGAN A type of grouse that lives in the tundra. Its white feathers go brown and red in summer.
RAINFOREST Tropical forest made luxuriant by high temperatures and daily rainfall.
RELIEF Ups and downs of the land, shown on relief maps by contours, colours or modelling.
RIFT VALLEY Deep valley caused by the sinking of the land between two parallel faults.
SALTWATER Water from the sea; water in lakes and rivers has no salt in it.
SAVANNA Tropical grassland with scattered trees, found between the rainforests and deserts in Africa, South America, Asia and Australia.
SCRUB Land covered by stunted trees and shrubs.
SEDGE Grasslike plant with triangular stem that grows in marshes.
SNOW LINE Height above which there is permanent ice and snow on a mountain.
SOFTWOOD Timber from conifers; hardwood comes from deciduous trees and takes much longer to grow.
SPARTINA Kind of marsh grass that holds silt and builds up mud.
STEPPE Treeless grassy plain, particularly in Russia and Ukraine.
SWAMP Area of wet spongy land.
TEMPERATE Describes regions that are not too hot or too cold.
TREE LINE Height on the globe or on a mountain above which trees do not grow.
TROPICS Regions with warm or hot climate that lie north and south of the equator. They are bounded by two imaginary lines: the tropic of Cancer at $23\frac{1}{2}°$N and the tropic of Capricorn at $23\frac{1}{2}°$S.
TUNDRA Huge treeless plains in the Arctic and on the tip of South America. Tundra also occurs on mountains.
UNDERSTOREY Trees, saplings and shrubs that grow in a forest below the canopy.
VELD High grassy plains in South Africa with almost no trees.
WADI Desert river bed that is dry for most of the time.
WEATHERING Erosion by extremes of temperature and chemical action.
WETLANDS Areas of land that are almost submerged.

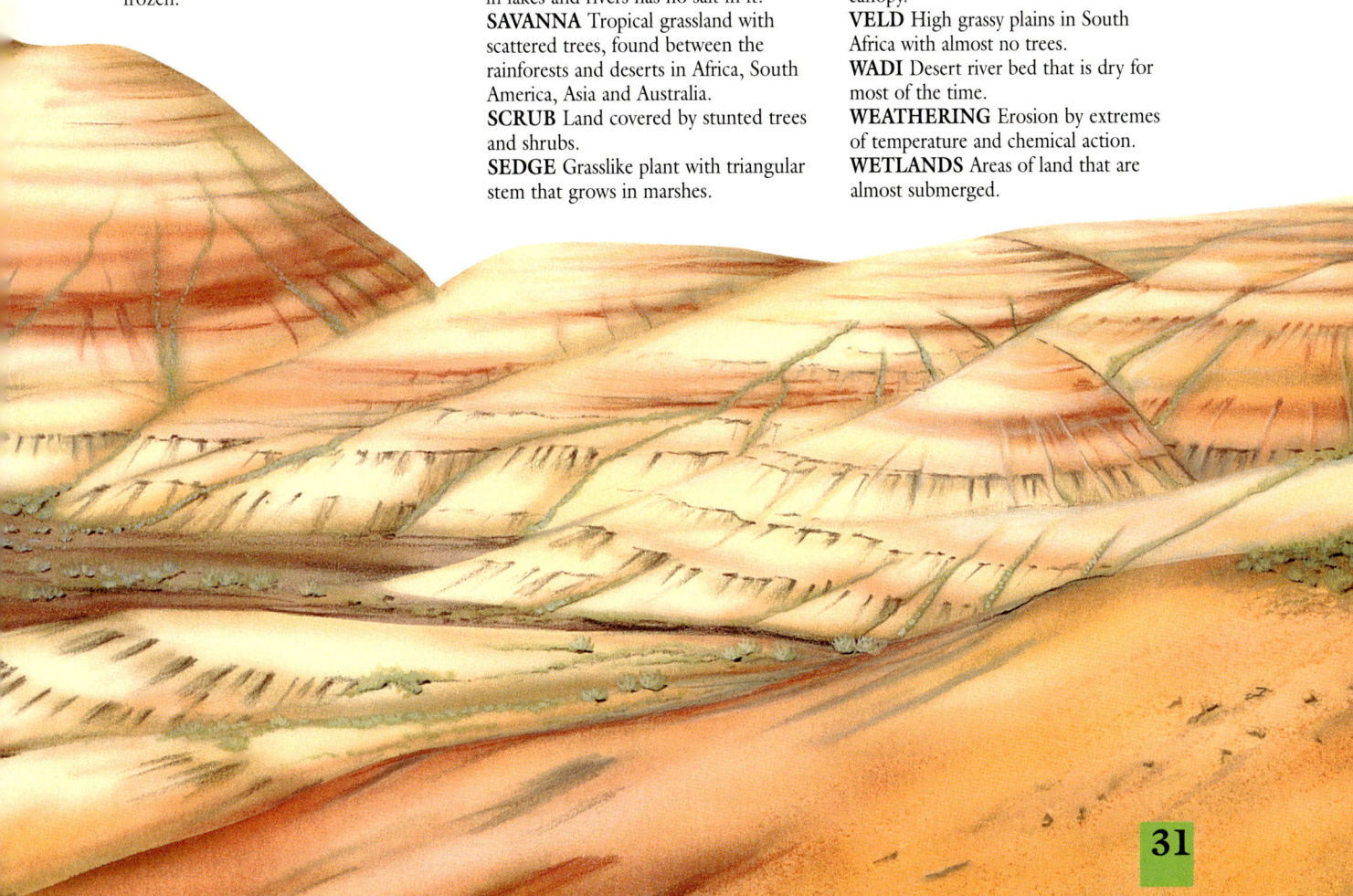

INDEX

Acacia trees 14, *14*, 15
Africa: deserts 16, *17*
   grasslands 18
   savanna *14*, 15
Altitude, effect on climate 11
Amazon rainforest 13
Animal species: desert: Sahara 10
   desert adaptations 17, *17*
   effect on landscape 4, *4*
   grasslands 18, 19
   importance of rainfall 11, *11*
   protected habitats *24*
   rainforest 13
   savanna 15, *15*
   temperate forests 20
   tundra 22, 23, *23*
Arroyos 16
Asia: desert animals 17
   forests 20
   grasslands 18
   tundra 22
Atacama desert 16

Baobab trees 14, *14*
Beaches, how they form 9, 25
Bird species: grassland 19
   rainforest species 13
   tundra 23
   wetlands 24
Block mountains 7
Bogs 24
Boreal forest 21, *21*
Brazilian rainforest 13

Cactuses 16
Cave formation 8
Cliffs 8
Climate: and rainfall 10, *10*
   during ice ages 10
   effect on landscape 4, 5, 11
   see also Temperature
Coasts: climate 11
   erosion 8
   landscape *2*
Coniferous woodland 20, 21, *21*
Cork oak 20, *20*

Deciduous woodland 20, 21
Deserts 9
   formation of 10, 11

Earth: timescale 5, *5*
   movement of plates 6-7, *7*
Earthquakes, how they happen 7
Epiphytes 12
Equatorial climate 11
Erosion: how it happens 6, *6*
Europe: forests 20
   tundra 22

Farmland, creation of 26, *26*
   on grasslands 19, *19*
Faults 7
Fen 24
Fires, savanna 15, 27
Fish species, Amazon river 13
Flash floods 16
Fold mountains 6
Fossils, study of 5
Freshwater wetlands 24
Frost, effect on landscape 6
Funnel-shaped valley *9*

Glaciers 9
Grass: prairie 18, *18*

savanna 14, 15
Grasslands, tropical 14-15, *14-15*

Hills, flat-topped 9
Human beings: effect on landscape 4, *4*, 26, *26*
   evolution 5
   threat to tundra 23
Humus 18

Ice, effect of: in tundra 22, *22*
   on landscape 6, 8
Insect species: desert 17
   grassland 19
   rainforest 13

Lakes: formation of 7
   wetland 24
Landscape, what it is 4-5, *4-5*
Lava 7
Lianas 12

Mangrove swamps 25
Mediterranean woodlands 20
Mesozoic era 5, *5*
Migrations: savannas 15
   tundra 23
   white storks 24
Mountains: climate 11
   erosion of 6
   formation of 6-7, *6-7*
   making models 28-9, *28-9*
Mudflats 25

North America: desert animals *17*
   forests 20
   grasslands 18, *18*
   tundra 22
Nutrients: rainforest soils 13
   savanna soils 15

Oasis 17
Ocean currents, and climate 11
Orchids 12

Palaeozoic era 5, *5*
Pampas 18
Peat 24
Permafrost 22, *22*
Plant species: desert 16, *16*, 17
   drought evaders 16
   importance of rainfall 11, *11*
   marshes 24
   rainforests 12-13, *12-13*
   Sahara desert 10
   saltwater wetlands 25
   savanna 14-15, *14-15*
   tundra 22, 23, *22*
Polar regions, climate 10
Prairies 18-19, *18-19*
   summer/winter *19*
Precambrian era 5, *5*

Rain, effect of: deserts 9
   landscape 6, *6*
Rainfall: 17
   climate and 10, *10*
   coastal 11
   deserts 16
   effect on grasslands 18
   importance of 11, *11*
   prairie 19
   rainforest 26
Rainforests 11
   destruction of 26, *26*

making your own 29, *29*
   what it is 12, *12*
Rainy season, savanna 15, *15*
Rift valley 7
Rivers: erosion by 6, *6-7*, 9, *9*
   ice *see* Glaciers
Rock cycle 7
Rocks: determining age 5
   effect of erosion 8, *8*
   in deserts 9
   effect on landscape 4, *4*
   formation of new 7
   glacial 9
   particles *see* Sand; Sediment

Sahara 10, *10*, 16
Saltwater wetlands 25, *25*
Sand, erosion by 9
Sand dunes: coastal 9
   desert 11, 16
   formation of 9
Seasons: grasslands *19*
   savannas 14, 15, *15*
   temperate forests 21, *21*
   tundra 23, *23*
Sediment 6, 9
Soil: bogs and fens 24
   formation in wetlands 25
   prairie 19
   rainforest 13, 26, *26*
   savanna 15
   steppes 19
   tundra 22, *22*
South America: desert 16
   grasslands 18
   rainforest 13
   savanna *14*
Springs 17
Steppes 18, *18*
Streams, underground 17
Sun, and climate 10, *10*

Temperate forests 20, *20*
Temperature: deserts 16
   distance from equator and 10, *10*
   savanna 14
   tundra 22
Trees: clearance of 20, *20*
   grassland 18
   rainforest 12-13, *12-13*
   savanna 14, *14*
   temperate forests 20, *20-1*
Tropical climate 10, *10*
Tundra 22-23, *22-23*

Valleys: desert 16
   how they are formed 9, *9*
   U-shaped 9
   V-shaped 9
Veld 18
Volcanoes, where they happen 7

Wadis 16
Water: effect on climate 11
   effect on deserts 16
   erosion model 28, *28*
   in deserts *see* Oasis
   see also Rivers
Wells 17
Wetlands 24-5, *24-5*
Wind, effect of: deserts 16
   erosion by 8, *8*
   desert formation 11
   landscape 6, 8, *8*